BETTER TOGETHER: ANIMAL GROUPS

LION PRIDES

by Karen Latchana Kenney

pogo

Ideas for Parents and Teachers

Pogo Books let children practice reading informational text while introducing them to nonfiction features such as headings, labels, sidebars, maps, and diagrams, as well as a table of contents, glossary, and index.

Carefully leveled text with a strong photo match offers early fluent readers the support they need to succeed.

Before Reading

- "Walk" through the book and point out the various nonfiction features. Ask the student what purpose each feature serves.
- Look at the glossary together. Read and discuss the words.

Read the Book

- Have the child read the book independently.
- Invite him or her to list questions that arise from reading.

After Reading

- Discuss the child's questions. Talk about how he or she might find answers to those questions.
- Prompt the child to think more. Ask: Lions are apex predators. But they still benefit from living in prides. Can you think of other apex predators that live in groups?

Pogo Books are published by Jump!
5357 Penn Avenue South
Minneapolis, MN 55419
www.jumplibrary.com

Library of Congress Cataloging-in-Publication Data

Names: Kenney, Karen Latchana, author.
Title: Lion prides / by Karen Latchana Kenney.
Description: Pogo books edition.
Minneapolis, MN: Jump!, Inc., [2020] |
Series: Better together: animal groups
Audience: Age 7–10. | Includes index.
Identifiers: LCCN 2019009393 (print)
LCCN 2019010578 (ebook)
ISBN 9781641288521 (ebook)
ISBN 9781641288514 (hardcover : alk. paper)
Subjects: LCSH: Lion–Behavior–Juvenile literature.
Animal societies–Juvenile literature.
Classification: LCC QL737.C23 (ebook)
LCC QL737.C23 K466 2020 (print)
DDC 599.75/5156–dc23
LC record available at https://lccn.loc.gov/2019009393

Editor: Jenna Trnka
Designer: Jenna Casura

Photo Credits: Linda Caldwell/Alamy, cover; kovop58/iStock, 1; Greg Lightle/Shutterstock, 3; Gerry van der Walt/Shutterstock, 4; Minden Pictures/SuperStock, 5 (background); Byrdyak/iStock, 5 (foreground); Cheryl Ramalho/iStock, 6-7; DENIS-HUOT Michel/Hemis/SuperStock, 8-9; Tony Campbell/Shutterstock, 10-11 (lion); Joe McDonald/Shutterstock, 10-11 (cheetah); Lingbeek/iStock, 12; Jurgens Potgieter/Shutterstock, 13 (buffalo); Anky/Shutterstock, 13 (lion); Suzi Eszterhas/Minden Pictures/SuperStock, 14-15, 16-17; Kirill Dorofeev/Shutterstock, 18; ANDREYGUDKOV/iStock, 19; Biosphoto/SuperStock, 20-21; jez_bennett/iStock, 23.

Printed in the United States of America at Corporate Graphics in North Mankato, Minnesota.

TABLE OF CONTENTS

CHAPTER 1

A CLOSE FAMILY

It is **dusk** in the African **savanna**. A lion stands tall and roars. It can be heard five miles (8 kilometers) away!

She is calling to her **pride**. Members of the pride are nearby. They roar back. This group lives, hunts, and eats together. Being together helps the lions survive.

Prides are lion families. Most prides have at least 15 lions. There are a few adult males. These males **mate** with the females. Adult females and their young make up the rest of the pride.

The lions **bond** with one another. How? They lick each other's fur. Why? This keeps it clean. They tumble and play, too. They pretend to hunt. They rub heads and snuggle. They are a close family group.

DID YOU KNOW?

Lions are the only cats that live in groups. Other cats live alone.

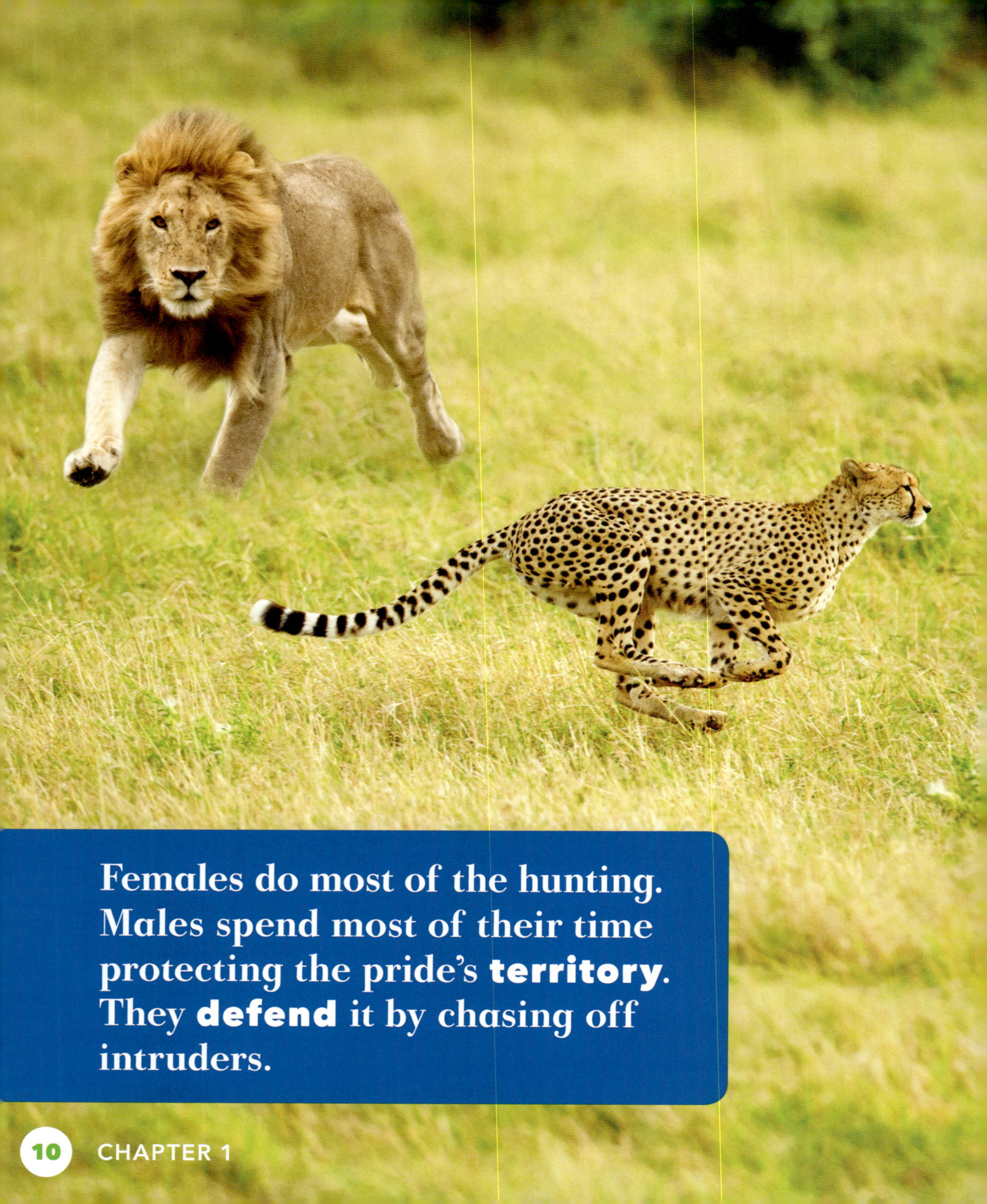

Females do most of the hunting. Males spend most of their time protecting the pride's **territory**. They **defend** it by chasing off intruders.

TAKE A LOOK!

Most lions live in Africa. Take a look at where!

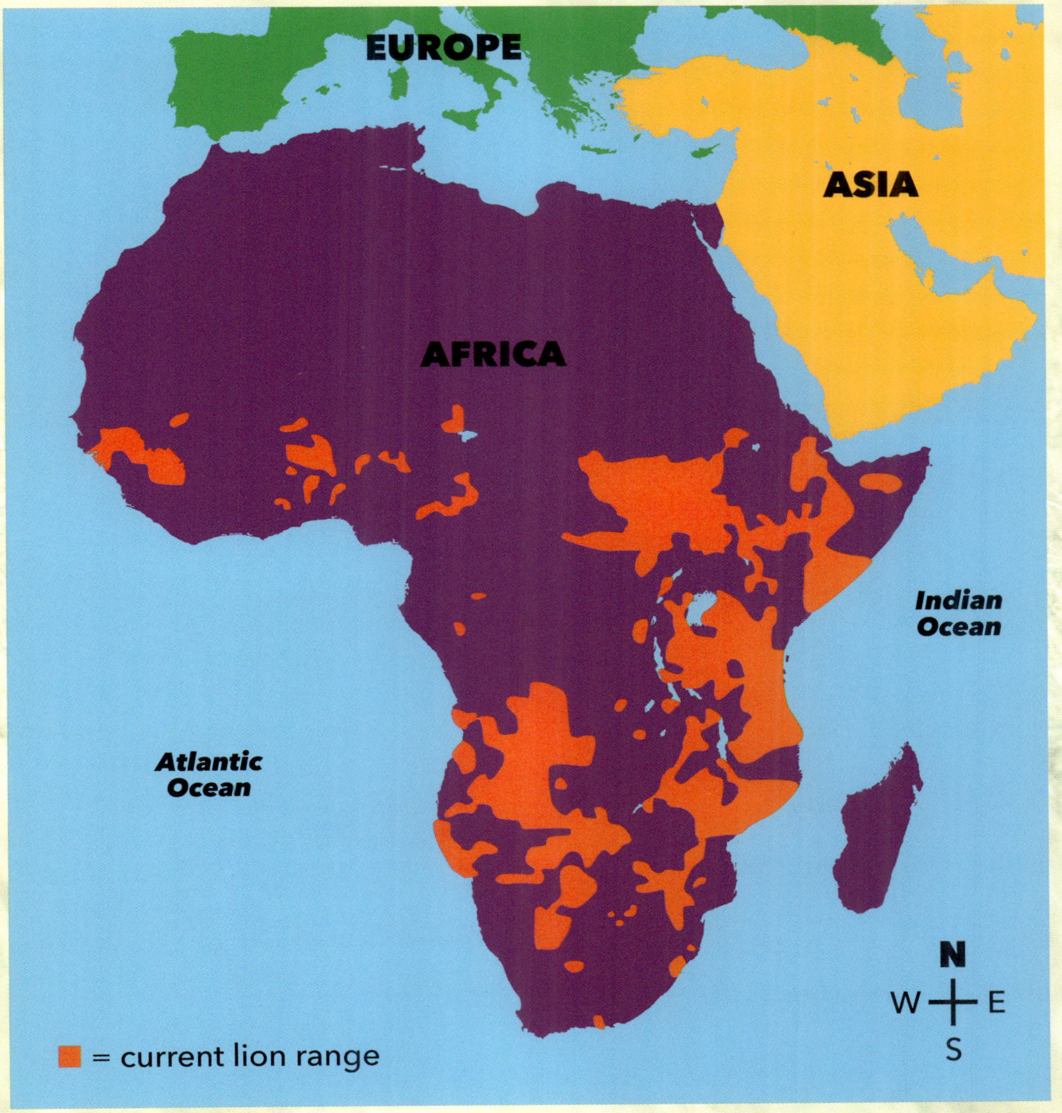

CHAPTER 2

SNEAKY HUNTERS

Lions are strong and fierce **apex predators**. They are at the top of their **food chain**. They eat buffalo, antelope, wildebeests, zebras, and even hippos. Sometimes they catch giraffes and elephants, too.

African buffalo

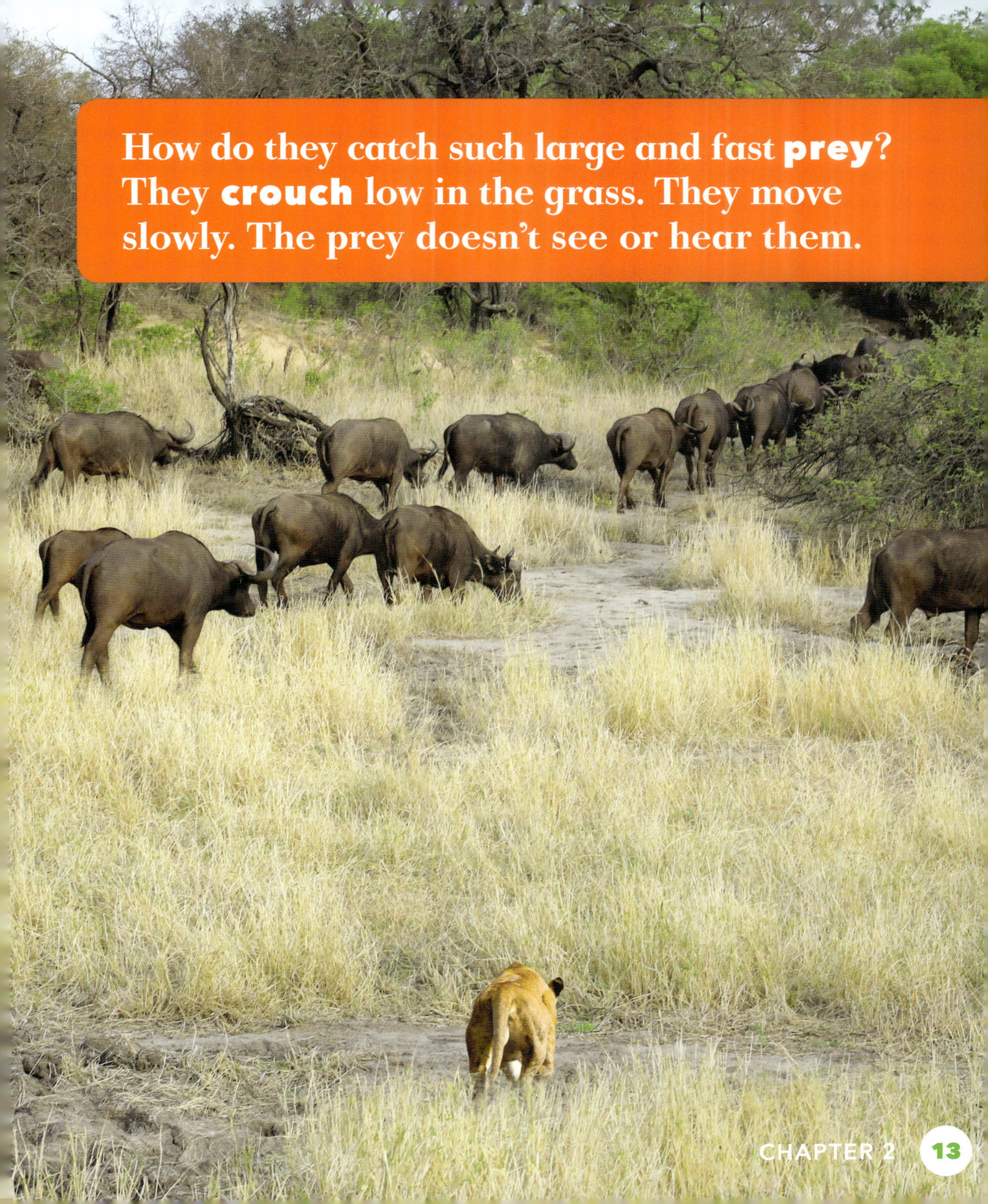

How do they catch such large and fast **prey**? They **crouch** low in the grass. They move slowly. The prey doesn't see or hear them.

Lions can't run fast for long. Their prey is often faster. So how do they catch their prey? Members of the pride work together.

DID YOU KNOW?

Lions have great **vision**. It is at least six times better than human vision! This helps them hunt at dusk or at night.

Members of the pride gang up on one buffalo. They leap onto the prey. They bite its neck. When it dies, all of the lions eat. The pride shares the meal.

DID YOU KNOW?

Even though the females do most of the hunting, the males get to eat first. Then the females eat. **Cubs** eat last. Lions eat a lot at each meal. They eat so much that they can eat just once a week.

CHAPTER 3

NEWEST MEMBERS OF THE PRIDE

Many cubs are in one pride. They are all born around the same time.

Their eyelids are closed for about three weeks. During that time, the cubs are completely **dependent** on their mothers.

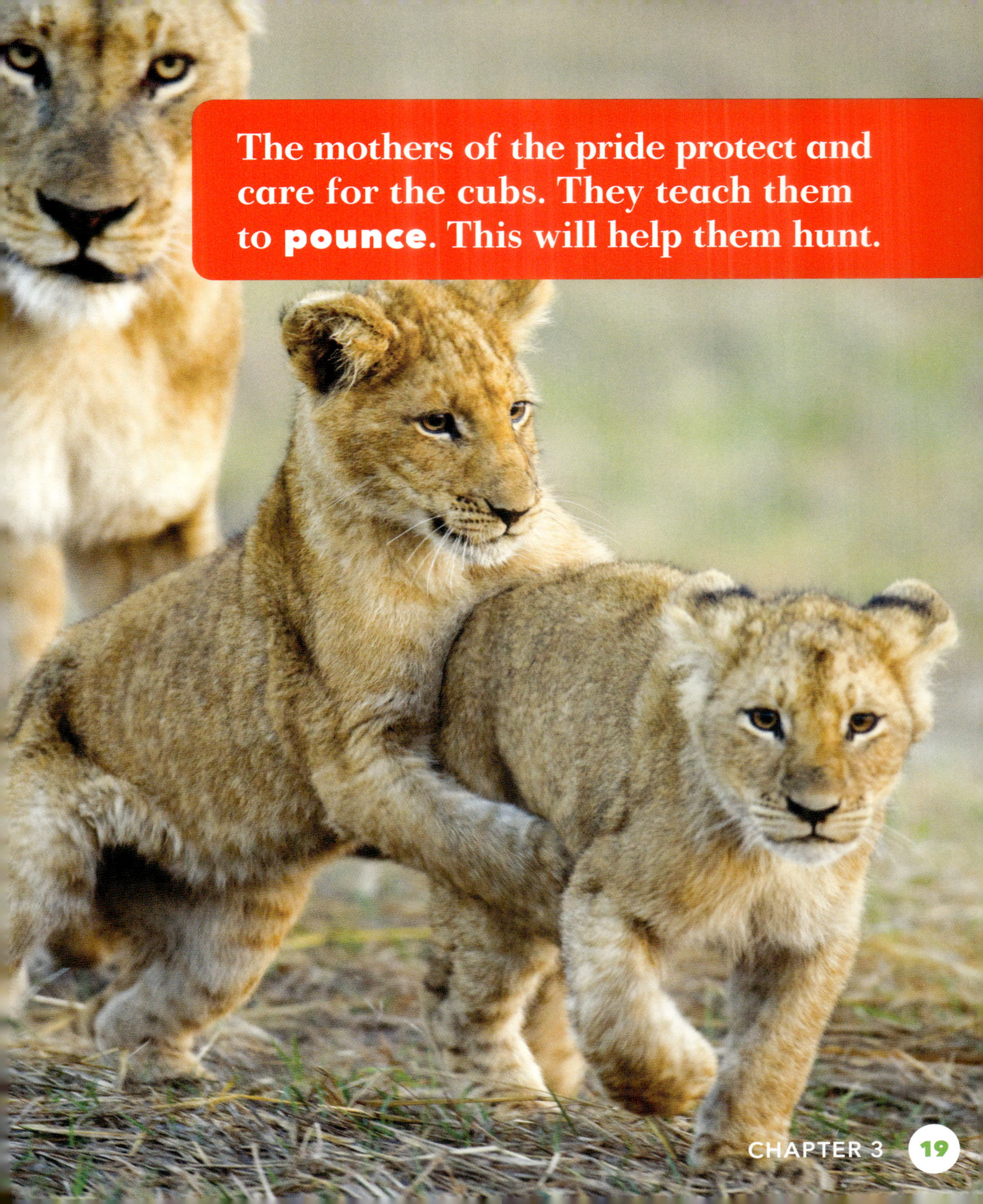

The mothers of the pride protect and care for the cubs. They teach them to **pounce**. This will help them hunt.

The new cubs play with each other. They copy the adults in the pride. They pretend to fight and hunt. As they grow, they learn how to be part of the pride. They hunt together. They eat together. They keep each other safe.

ACTIVITIES & TOOLS

TRY THIS!

DRAW YOUR OWN FOOD CHAIN

Lions are at the top of the African savanna food chain. They eat zebras, antelope, wildebeests, giraffes, and many other larger animals. These animals eat grasses.

Ask a librarian or other trusted adult to help you look up other food chains or webs. Draw one. Which plants or animals are at the bottom? What animal, or apex predator, is at the top of that food chain?

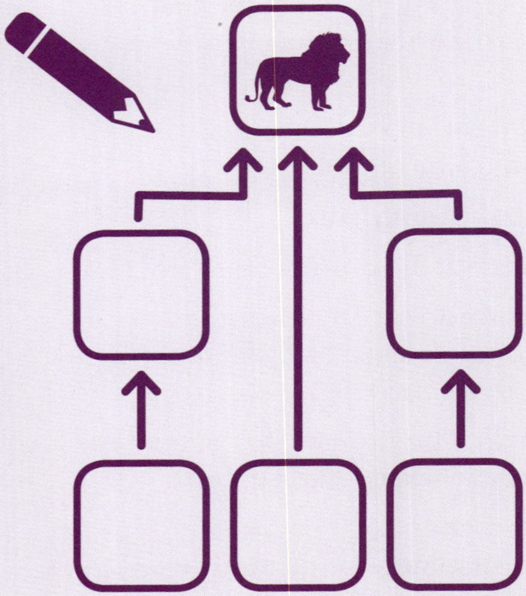

GLOSSARY

apex predators: Predators at the top of a food chain that are not hunted by any other animal.

bond: To form a close connection or strong feelings toward one another.

crouch: To bend the legs and lower the body.

cubs: Young lions.

defend: To protect from harm.

dependent: Depending on and taken care of by something or someone else.

dusk: The time of day after sunset when it starts getting dark.

food chain: An ordered arrangement of animals and plants in which each feeds on the one below it in the chain.

mate: To join together to produce babies.

pounce: To jump forward and grab something suddenly.

prey: Animals that are hunted by other animals for food.

pride: A group of lions that consists of adult males and females and their cubs.

savanna: A flat, grassy plain with few or no trees.

territory: An area of land a group of animals lives in and protects.

vision: The sense of sight.

INDEX

TO LEARN MORE

Finding more information is as easy as 1, 2, 3.

1. Go to www.factsurfer.com
2. Enter "lionprides" into the search box.
3. Choose your book to see a list of websites.